MW00877508

The Worship Series

Volume 1

Beginner Hymns with Teacher Duets

Arrangements by

Pam Turner

pam turner piano

www.pamturnerpiano.com

The Worship Series Volume 1
Beginner Hymns with Teacher Duets

Arrangements by Pam Turner

ISBN 978-1721782055

Pam Turner Piano

www.pamturnerpiano.com

The Worship Series

Volume 1

Beginner Hymns with Teacher Duets

What a Friend We Have in Jesus..................................1

Come, Thou Fount of Every Blessing.....................3

Just As I Am 5

Jesus Loves Me...7

I Surrender All...9

Sweet Hour of Prayer 11

Trust and Obey 15

Praise Him, Praise Him.................................... 19

Heavenly Sunlight 23

Nearer My God to Thee 27

Arrangements by Pam Turner

www.pamturnerpiano.com

1. What a Friend We Have in Jesus

(Teacher Duet)

Charles C. Converse
Arr. Pam Turner

1. What a Friend We Have in Jesus

"Now you are my friends, since I have told you everything the Father told me." John 15:15

Charles C. Converse
Arr. Pam Turner

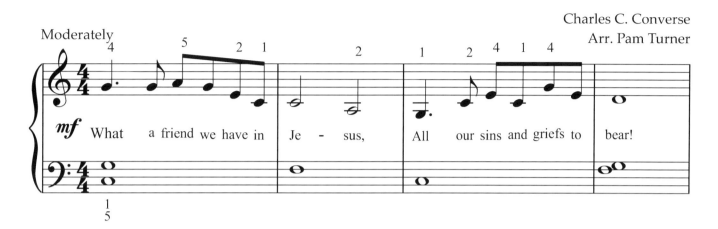

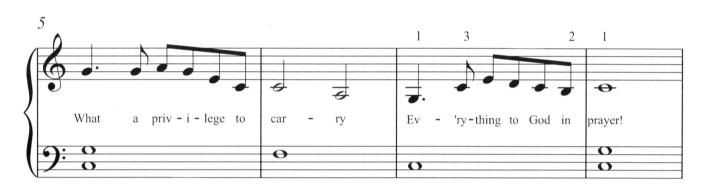

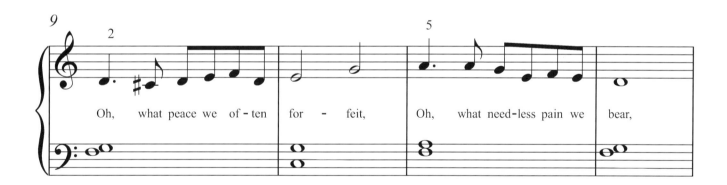

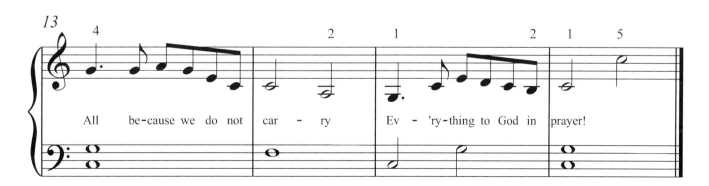

2. Come, Thou Fount of Every Blessing

(Teacher Duet)

Traditional
Arr. Pam Turner

Moderately
Teacher intro:

Student part two octaves higher

* *Student upbeats*

2. Come, Thou Fount of Every Blessing

"Whatever is good and perfect is a gift coming down to us from God our Father..." James 1:17

Traditional
Arr. Pam Turner

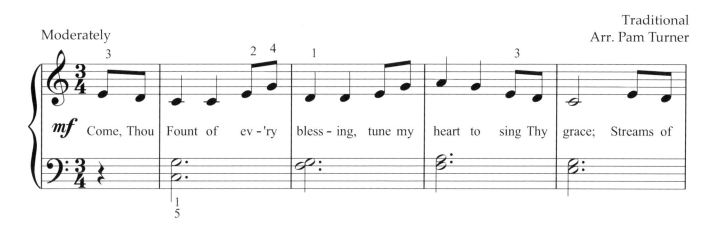

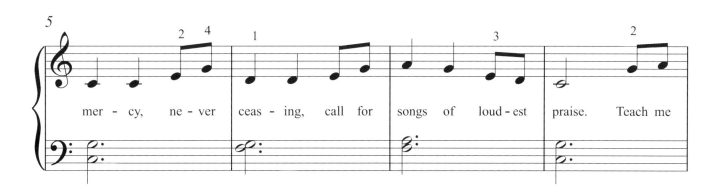

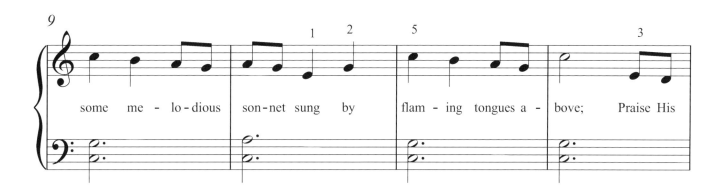

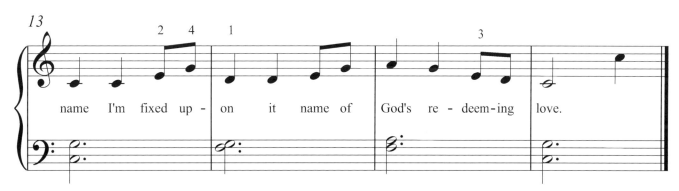

5

3. Just As I Am

"Come to me, all of you who are weary...and I will give you rest." Matthew 11:28

William B. Bradbury
Arr. Pam Turner

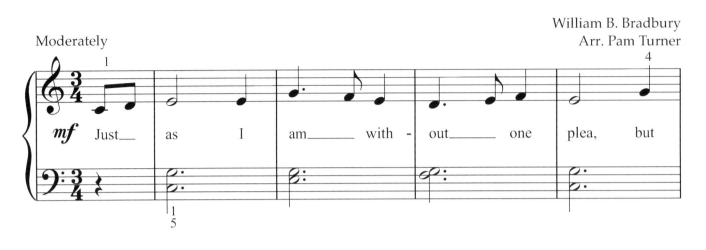

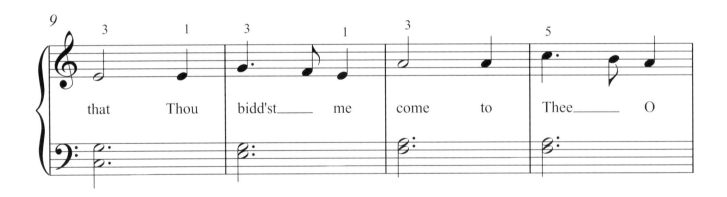

3. Just as I Am

(Teacher Duet)

William B. Bradbury
Arr. Pam Turner

Moderately
Teacher intro:

Student part as written

*Student upbeats

4. Jesus Loves Me

(Teacher Duet)

William B. Bradbury
Arr. Pam Turner

4. Jesus Loves Me

"I have loved you even as the Father has loved me." John 15:9

William B. Bradbury
Arr. Pam Turner

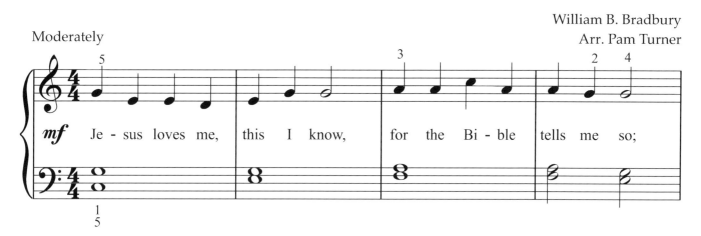

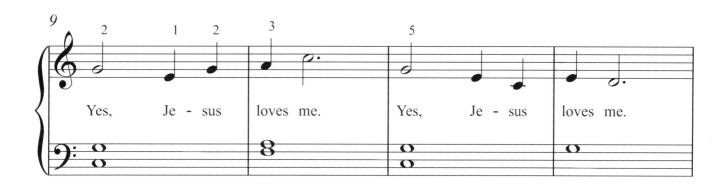

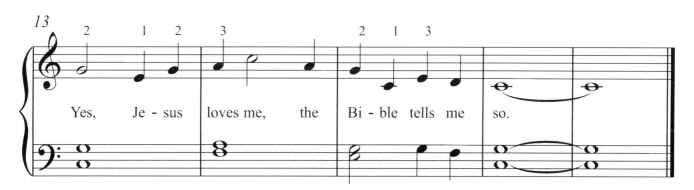

5. I Surrender All
(Teacher Duet)

Winfield S. Weeden
Arr. Pam Turner

Moderately
Teacher intro:

5. I Surrender All

"My old self has been crucified with Christ." Galatians 2:20

Winfield S. Weeden
Arr. Pam Turner

Moderately

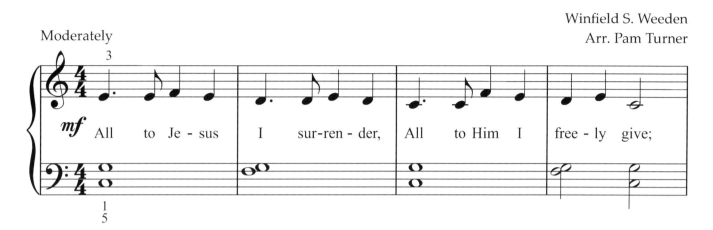

mf All to Je - sus I sur-ren - der, All to Him I free - ly give;

I will ev - er love and trust Him, in His pres-ence dai - ly live.

I sur-ren - der all, I sur-ren - der all; All to Thee, my

bles - sed Sav - ior, I sur-ren - der all.

6. Sweet Hour of Prayer

(Teacher Duet)

William B. Bradbury
Arr. Pam Turner

Moderately
Teacher intro:

*1 Student part two octaves higher

*Student upbeats

6. Sweet Hour of Prayer

"Devote yourselves to prayer with an alert mind and a thankful heart." Colossians 4:2

William B. Bradbury
Arr. Pam Turner

(Teacher Duet)

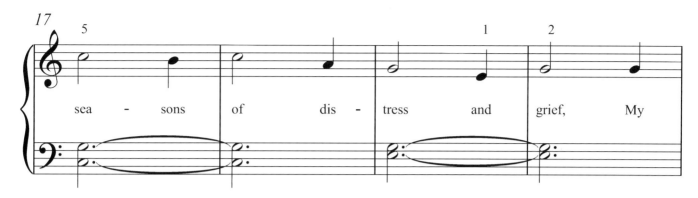

sea - sons of dis - tress and grief, My

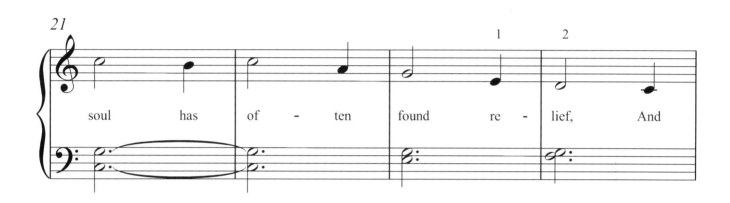

soul has of - ten found re - lief, And

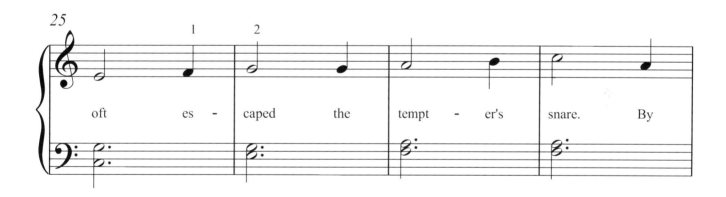

oft es - caped the tempt - er's snare. By

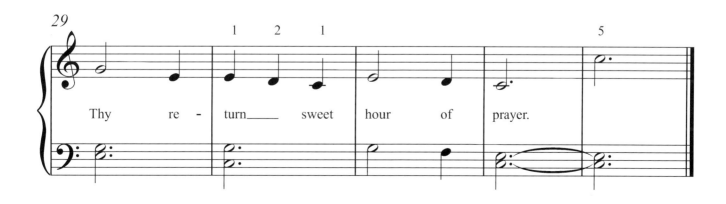

Thy re - turn____ sweet hour of prayer.

7. Trust and Obey

(Teacher Duet)

Daniel B. Towner
Arr. Pam Turner

*Student upbeats

7. Trust and Obey

"Commit your actions to the Lord, and your plans will succeed." Proverbs 16:3

Daniel B. Towner
Arr. Pam Turner

Moderately

When we walk with the Lord, in the

Light of His word, What a glo - ry He

sheds on our way! Let us do His good

will; He a - bides with us still, and with

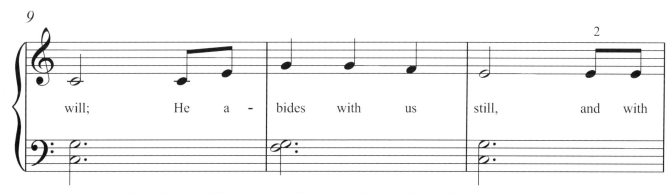

(Teacher Duet)

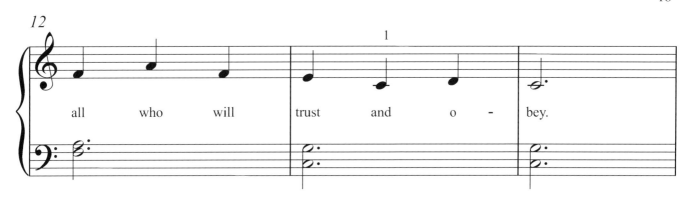

all   who   will   trust   and   o – bey.

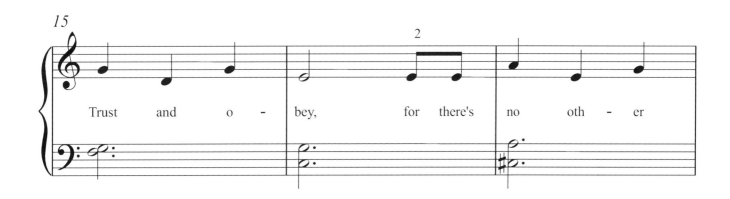

Trust   and   o – bey,   for   there's   no   oth – er

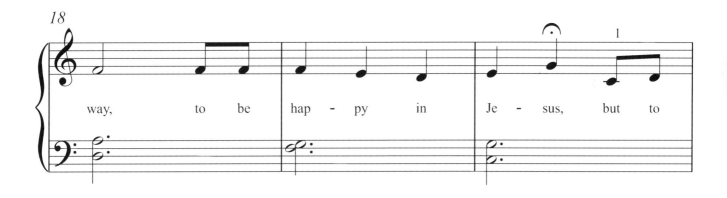

way,   to   be   hap – py   in   Je – sus,   but   to

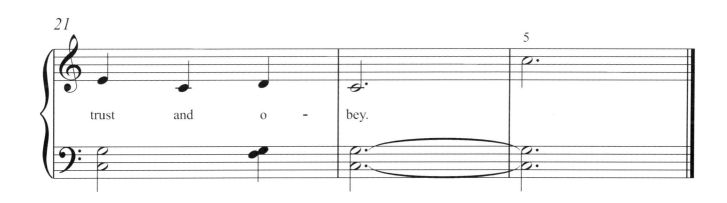

trust   and   o – bey.

8. Praise Him! Praise Him!

"How good to sing praises to our God!." Psalm 147:1

Chester G. Allen
Arr. Pam Turner

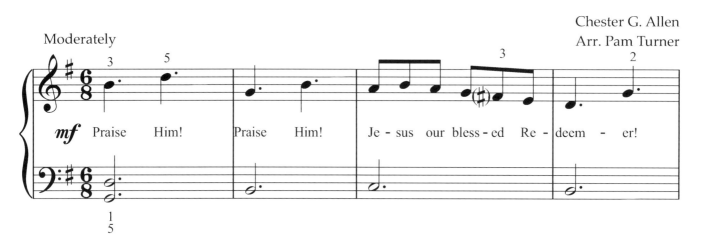

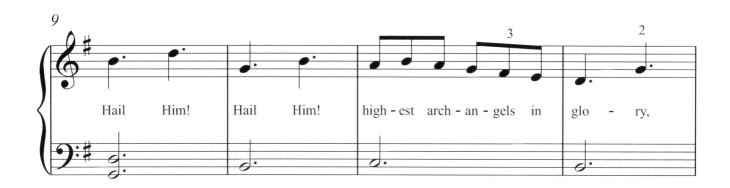

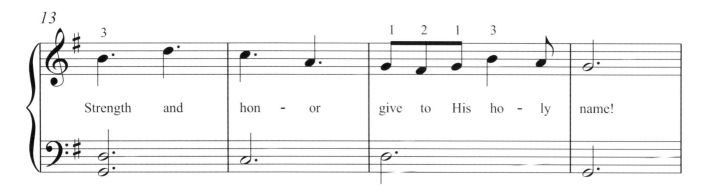

8. Praise Him! Praise Him!

(Teacher Duet)

Moderately

Student part as written
Both hands 8va

Chester G. Allen
Arr. Pam Turner

(Student Part)

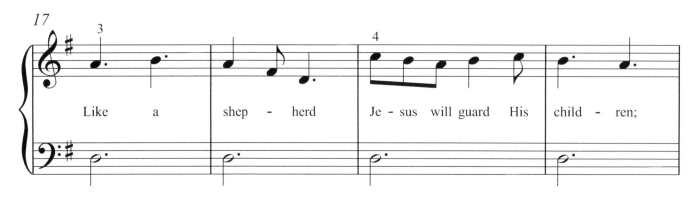

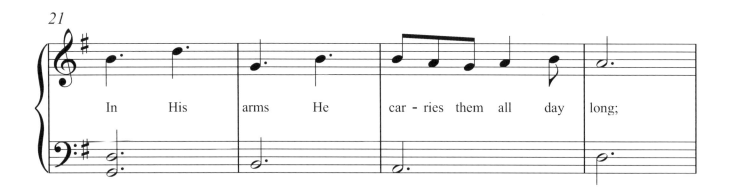

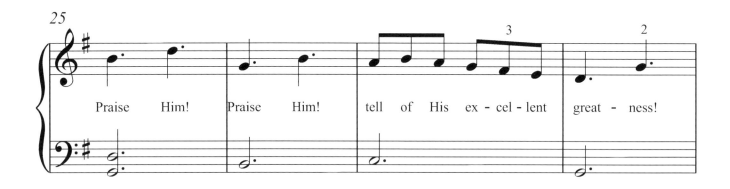

9. Heavenly Sunlight

(Teacher Duet)

Moderately

George Harrison Cook
Arr. Pam Turner

9. Heavenly Sunlight

"The Lord is my helper, so I will have no fear." Hebrews 13:6

George Harrison Cook
Arr. Pam Turner

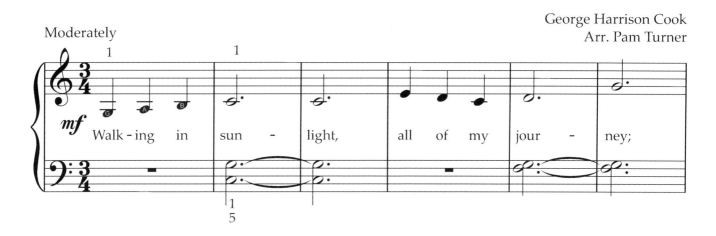

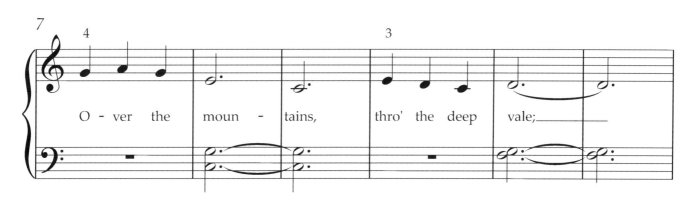

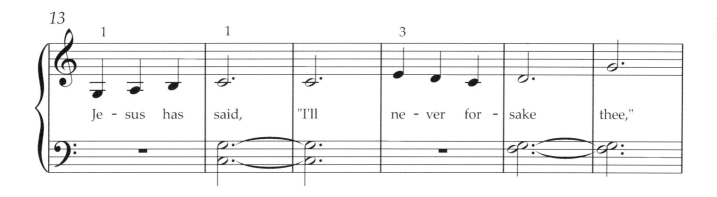

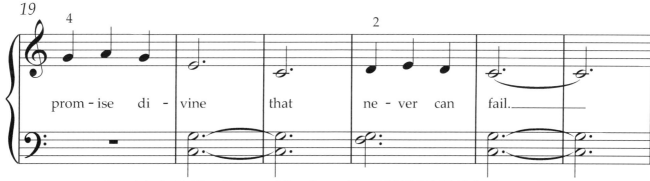

(Teacher Duet)

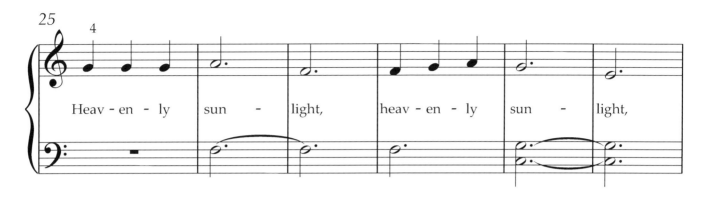

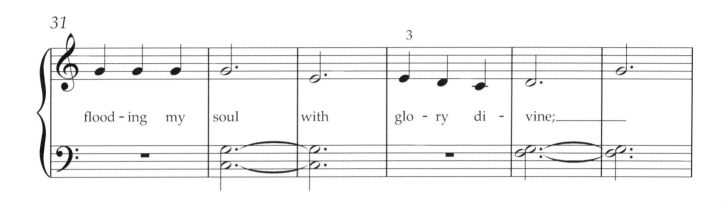

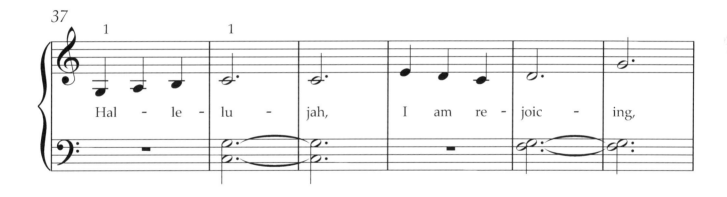

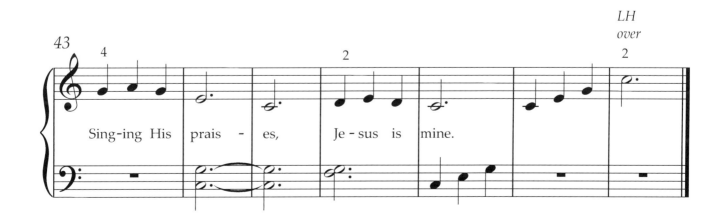

10. Nearer My God to Thee

(Teacher Duet)

Lowell Mason
Arr. Pam Turner

Moderately
Teacher intro:

Student part one octave higher

10. Nearer My God to Thee

"But you are near, O Lord, and all your commands are true." Psalm 119:151

Lowell Mason
Arr. Pam Turner

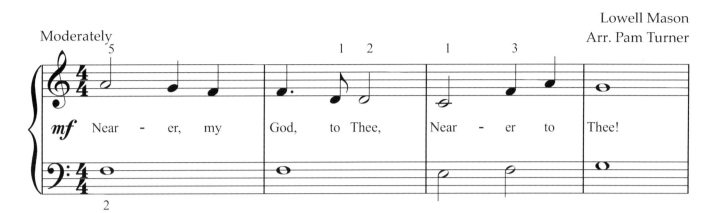

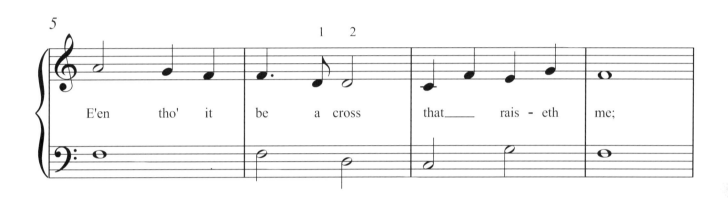

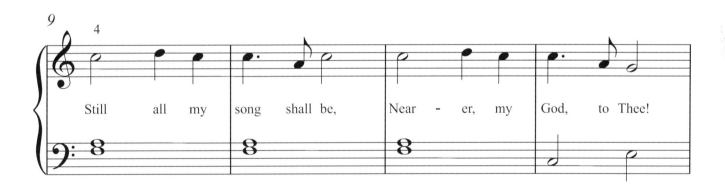

Made in the USA
Monee, IL
19 January 2022

89432826R00020